GW00731434

by George Forbes

WRITING *to* REMEMBER

Lang**Syne**

PUBLISHING

WRITING *to* REMEMBER

79 Main Street, Newtongrange,
Midlothian EH22 4NA
Tel: 0131 344 0414   Fax: 0845 075 6085
E-mail: info@lang-syne.co.uk
www.langsyneshop.co.uk

Design by Dorothy Meikle
Printed by Printwell Ltd
© Lang Syne Publishers Ltd 2017

ISBN 978-1-85217-090-5

Fraser

SEPT NAMES INCLUDE:
Cowie
Frew
Frissell
Frizell
Macgruer
Macimmey
Mackim
Mackimmie
Macsymon
Syme
Symon
Simpson
Tweedie

Fraser

MOTTO:
All my Hope is in God.

CREST:
A Strawberry Plant Proper.

TERRITORY:
Inverness-shire and
along the Beauly Firth.

Chapter one:

The origins of the clan system

by Rennie McOwan

The original Scottish clans of the Highlands and the great families of the Lowlands and Borders were gatherings of families, relatives, allies and neighbours for mutual protection against rivals or invaders.

Scotland experienced invasion from the Vikings, the Romans and English armies from the south. The Norman invasion of what is now England also had an influence on land-holding in Scotland. Some of these invaders stayed on and in time became 'Scottish'.

The word clan derives from the Gaelic language term 'clann', meaning children, and it was first used many centuries ago as communities were formed around tribal lands in glens and mountain fastnesses.

The format of clans changed over the centuries, but at its best the chief and his family held the land on behalf of all, like trustees, and the ordinary clansmen and women believed they had a blood relationship with the founder of their clan.

There were two way duties and obligations. An inadequate chief could be deposed and replaced by someone of greater ability.

Clan people had an immense pride in race. Their relationship with the chief was like adult children to a father and they had a real dignity.

The concept of clanship is very old and a more feudal notion of authority gradually crept in.

Pictland, for instance, was divided into seven principalities ruled by feudal leaders who were the strongest and most charismatic leaders of their particular groups.

By the sixth century the 'British' kingdoms of Strathclyde, Lothian and Celtic Dalriada (Argyll) had emerged and Scotland, as one nation, began to take shape in the time of King Kenneth MacAlpin.

Some chiefs claimed descent from

ancient kings which may not have been accurate in every case.

By the twelfth and thirteenth centuries the clans and families were more strongly brought under the central control of Scottish monarchs.

Lands were awarded and administered more and more under royal favour, yet the power of the area clan chiefs was still very great.

The long wars to ensure Scotland's independence against the expansionist ideas of English monarchs extended the influence of some clans and reduced the lands of others.

Those who supported Scotland's greatest king, Robert the Bruce, were awarded the territories of the families who had opposed his claim to the Scottish throne.

In the Scottish Borders country – the notorious Debatable Lands – the great families built up a ferocious reputation for providing warlike men accustomed to raiding into England and occasionally fighting one another.

Chiefs had the power to dispense justice and to confiscate lands and clan warfare produced a society where martial virtues – courage, hardiness, tenacity – were greatly admired.

Gradually the relationship between the clans and the Crown became strained as Scottish monarchs became more orientated to life in the Lowlands and, on occasion, towards England.

The Highland clans spoke a different language, Gaelic, whereas the language of Lowland Scotland and the court was Scots and in more modern times, English.

Highlanders dressed differently, had different customs, and their wild mountain land sometimes seemed almost foreign to people living in the Lowlands.

It must be emphasised that Gaelic culture was very rich and story-telling, poetry, piping, the clarsach (harp) and other music all flourished and were greatly respected.

Highland culture was different from other parts of Scotland but it was not inferior or less sophisticated.

Central Government, whether in London or Edinburgh, sometimes saw the Gaelic clans as

*"The spirit of the clan means much
to thousands of people"*

a challenge to their authority and some sent expeditions into the Highlands and west to crush the power of the Lords of the Isles.

Nevertheless, when the eighteenth century Jacobite Risings came along the cause of the Stuarts was mainly supported by Highland clans.

The word Jacobite comes from the Latin for James – Jacobus. The Jacobites wanted to restore the exiled Stuarts to the throne of Britain.

The monarchies of Scotland and England became one in 1603 when King James VI of Scotland (1st of England) gained the English throne after Queen Elizabeth died.

The Union of Parliaments of Scotland and England, the Treaty of Union, took place in 1707.

Some Highland clans, of course, and Lowland families opposed the Jacobites and supported the incoming Hanoverians.

After the Jacobite cause finally went down at Culloden in 1746 a kind of ethnic cleansing took place. The power of the chiefs was curtailed. Tartan and the pipes were banned in law.

Many emigrated, some because they

wanted to, some because they were evicted by force. In addition, many Highlanders left for the cities of the south to seek work.

Many of the clan lands became home to sheep and deer shooting estates.

But the warlike traditions of the clans and the great Lowland and Border families lived on, with their descendants fighting bravely for freedom in two world wars.

Remember the men from whence you came, says the Gaelic proverb, and to that could be added the role of many heroic women.

The spirit of the clan, of having roots, whether Highland or Lowland, means much to thousands of people.

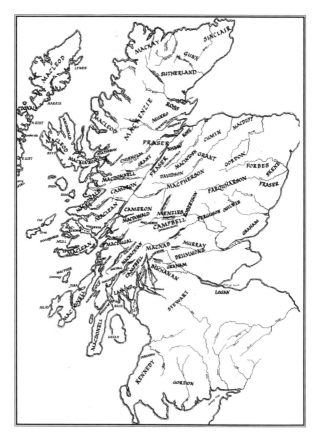

A map of the clans' homelands

Chapter two:

A race of heroes

The Frasers were descended from Norman knights in the Anjou district of France and their name comes from the French Freseau family who themselves originated in a savage tribe called the Friselii in Roman Gaul.

These warriors were once renowned for savagely fighting Julius Caesar's legions; thus establishing a military pedigree covering more than two thousand years, for the Frasers always were doughty fighters.

The French word 'fraise' means 'strawberry' and the Friselii tribal badge was the strawberry plant which grew abundantly in their territory.

One story tells how the Norman knight Julius de Berry of Bourbon entertained one of the French kings with a dish of these plump, juicy strawberries and so incurred his gastronomic delight that he ended up with a knighthood.

Presumably there was more to the latter than that
but a good table always helped.

Because of these connections, strawberries
were incorporated into the Fraser coat-of-arms,
where they have remained to this day.

The knights first settled in Tweedale in
the Borders in the mid-twelfth century and
gradually worked their way northwards,
gaining lands in East Lothian and finally

establishing strongholds in Inverness-shire and around the north-east coastline where the harbour refuge and township of Fraserburgh was eventually founded.

Sir Simon Fraser fought for both William Wallace and Robert the Bruce before being captured by the Hammer of the Scots, King Edward 1st, who had him brutally hanged, drawn and quartered, the dying patriot's only consolation being that he suffered the same horrific fate as his hero 'Braveheart'.

Sir Simon's cousin, Sir Alexander Fraser of Cowie, was Bruce's chamberlain and the elder brother of another Sir Simon from whom the Frasers of Lovat are descended.

He married Bruce's sister, Mary, who for months had been locked in a cage by the English and suspended from the walls of Roxburgh Castle, exposed to the bitter elements.

In 1375, a grandson of this match acquired the castle of Cairnbulg and the lands of Philorth in Buchan through marriage with Joanna, daughter of the Earl of Ross.

In the sixteenth century, it was Sir Alexander, the 8th Earl of Philorth, who founded Fraserburgh which became a major North Sea oil and fishing port; and he almost succeeded in setting up a university there but Aberdeen was not prepared to countenance a close academic rival just to the north.

Sir Alexander's son married the heiress of Saltoun, thus incorporating that title into the honours of future chiefs of his clan and into their heraldry.

When the bubonic plague struck Aberdeen in 1647, the staff and students from King's College were evacuated to Fraserburgh for two years: but now only a street name and some lettering carved on a wall are all that remain of this early seat of learning.

Sir Alexander Fraser of Durris was the personal physician of 'the merry monarch', Charles II. Educated at Aberdeen, Fraser soon acquired a reputation for a broad scholarship, especially in medicine.

He accompanied Charles throughout

his campaign in 1650 but incurred the displeasure of some of the more devout Royalists by his progressive scientific opinions, many of which were deemed heretical and even atheistical in that more blinkered era.

After the Restoration of Charles to the throne in 1660, Fraser sat in the Scottish Parliament, though he was still prominent in court circles down in London, to such an extent that he even featured in the diaries of Samuel Pepys.

Other branches of the Fraser family also prospered. Andrew Fraser of Muchalls was raised to the peerage in June, 1633, with the title Lord Fraser.

He completed the early work on Castle Fraser which stands south of the River Don near Inverurie. This magnificent keep, suitably reminiscent of a French chateau, is now fully renovated and is in the care of the National Trust for Scotland.

*Clan warfare produced a society where
courage and tenacity were greatly admired*

Chapter three:

The field of the shirts

A young MacDonald of Clanranald was brought up at the Fraser stronghold of Castle Dounie but unexpectedly became leader of his redoubtable Highland clan.

He proved a sore disappointment, being both tactless and lacking in any leadership qualities. He even criticised the numbers of cattle and goats killed for his inauguration feast and remarked that "a few hens would have done as well!"

He was duly ostracised by his offended clansmen for whom hospitality was a cardinal virtue, being nicknamed 'Ranald of the Hens'; and was sent packing back to his friends and protectors, the Frasers, who needed little excuse to take up arms in his support to quell a rival clan who had been raiding their lands and stealing cattle.

Both sides clashed beside Loch Lochy

on a swelteringly hot July day and, because the warriors threw off their plaids in the heat, the battle came to be known as 'Blar na Leine' or 'The Field of the Shirts'.

It was a ferocious encounter and the grass was soon scarlet with blood as hundreds were mown down by claymores. It was said that by the finish there were only around ten exhausted, wounded men left standing on either side.

The result was bloody indeed but tragically inconclusive.

The Frasers as a renowned fighting clan were never far away whenever there were scraps brewing in their neighbourhood. They often rallied to the colours, though this could sometimes lead to divided loyalties.

When the Stuarts were deposed and William of Orange sat on the throne, Lord Tullibardine raised a body of Atholl men which included 300 Frasers in support of the new ruler.

They paraded at Blair Castle and when their leaders addressed them it was then that the Frasers realised for the first time that they were supposed to be supporting King William.

They promptly fell out of the parade and made for the nearest burn where, Jacobites to a man, they filled their bonnets with water and drank a toast to the exiled King James, only regretting in true Highland fashion that there was nothing stronger to hand.

Then off they went to follow John Graham of Claverhouse, 'Bonnie Dundee', who led them to victory at the Pass of Killiecrankie when the Frasers were in the forefront of those who made that famous Highland charge down the purple glenside to rout the government forces in battle below as the sun set redly.

It was a sad victory for the Frasers, however, for their leader, Claverhouse, fell from his horse, a freak musket ball having been shot through his chest, later dying in the arms of his weeping followers. With him died this particular revolt: but there were others.

*They filled their bonnets with water and
drank a toast to the exiled King James*

Chapter four:

The Old Fox

Simon Fraser, the 12th Lord Lovat, earned for himself several disparaging nicknames, including 'the Old Fox' and 'the Wicked Rebel'.

All his life he was in and out of trouble and ended up being the last man beheaded by the axe in Britain.

His problems began when he was made clan chief because he was not entitled to the honour, being only his father's third son.

He took over by violence and guile. After his father got the title in 1696, Simon captured the daughter of the 10th Lord Lovat who had recently died (little Emelia was only nine but she was an heiress and that was all that mattered).

That done, he tried to marry her mother. He was refused so he raped the still grieving widow and forcibly married her. This marriage opened up his bid for the chieftainship.

Naturally, his wife's family, the Murrays of Atholl, were up in arms. They put the law onto him and he was found guilty of treason and condemned to death.

He fled 'over the sea' to Skye and then to France, thus establishing an escape route to be used by a more distinguished successor.

During this time in 1699 his father died, giving him his cherished ambition to lead the Clan Fraser.

As he cheated in his private life, so he cheated in politics. All his life he was for the Jacobites – and against them!

He started off his chequered national career by raising 300 Frasers for King William of Orange.

Then, five years later, he was over in France plotting with King Louis to put the Stuarts back on the throne.

The French trusted him but the Scottish Jacobites more shrewdly did not: but not even they realised he was acting as a secret agent for the British Government, passing back information to Whitehall.

When the 1715 Rebellion broke out, he stopped his clan from joining the Old Pretender's cause which left the Jacobites seriously weakened and contributed to the failure of the revolt.

Fraser's reward was a Royal Pardon and the granting of some of his lands back.

When the '45 Rebellion erupted, again he declared himself for the Government and against the Stuarts: but secretly he rallied his clan to Bonnie Prince Charlie's banner, even sending his 19-year-old son to lead them.

Fraser wanted to be on the winning side – he just was not sure what that would turn out to be.

But after the Jacobite victory at Prestonpans, he openly showed his hand and said he and his men were for the Prince.

It was a bad mistake for, after the debacle of Culloden, he found himself on the run in the Highland heather, though, old and ill, he had to be carried much of the time by faithful retainers.

He was eventually cornered on an island in Loch Morar and taken down in chains to the House of Lords in London where a swift trial ended with a guilty verdict.

On a cold, rainy morning on Thursday, April 9th, 1747, a huge crowd gathered at Tower Hill to watch the end of the obese, crippled, 80-year-old clan chief.

Rather like Charles I, Fraser's finest moment was also his last. He showed great courage and coolness, even managing to crack a joke with his executioner, pulling out a purse of gold coins and giving it to the grim axeman with the words:

"Here, sir, is ten guineas for you. Pray do your work well, for if you should cut and hack my shoulders and I should be able to rise again, I should be angry with you!"

However, the axeman did as he was bid and swung his weapon so hard that it buried itself two inches into the wooden block.

Succeeding Frasers redeemed the reputation of the family. Indeed, Fraser's own son, also called Simon (along with Hugh it was the most popular first name), after he had received a pardon for his Jacobite acitivities went on to raise 1,800 men who formed themselves into the Fraser Highlanders in 1757.

They fought valiantly for the British in America; and, as the General in charge, Simon was in command when his men defeated French troops and captured Quebec. A later clansman explored and named the Fraser River in Canada.

Many Frasers distinguished themselves under Wellington during the Napoleonic Wars.

They fought at Waterloo and it was a Fraser who drew the Duke's attention to Napoleon's Old Guard as they came up the hill to their doom in the final moments of that decisive battle.

And in more modern times the Lovat Scouts, led by and mostly comprising Highland Frasers, have fought as commandos in both World Wars of last century, as well as in the earlier Boer War.

Since their ranks were made up mostly of gamekeepers, stalkers and ghillies, these Scouts were renowned as sharpshooters and used their tracking skills to infiltrate behind enemy lines, performing many acts of valour in highly dangerous circumstances.

Again it was that old martial Fraser blood coming to the fore, just as it had done two millennia ago in the dark forests of Gaul.

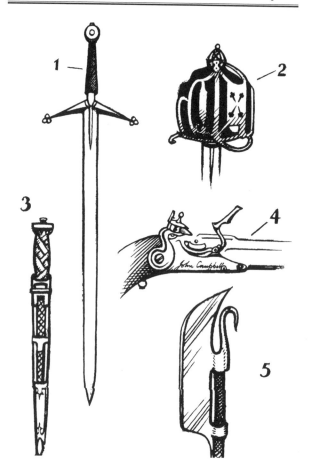

Highland weapons

1) The claymore or two-handed sword
   (fifteenth or early sixteenth century)

2) Basket hilt of broadsword
   made in Stirling, 1716

3) Highland dirk
   (eighteenth century)

4) Steel pistol *(detail)* made in Doune

5) Head of Lochaber Axe as carried
   in the '45 and earlier